ETERNAL SENTENCES

Miller Williams Poetry Series
EDITED BY BILLY COLLINS

ETERNAL SENTENCES

MICHAEL McGRIFF

The University of Arkansas Press
Fayetteville
2021

ISBN: 978-1-68226-162-0
eISBN: 978-1-61075-741-6

Manufactured in the United States of America

25 24 23 22 21   5 4 3 2 1

Designed by Liz Lester

♾ The paper used in this publication meets the minimum requirements
of the American National Standard for Permanence of Paper for Printed
Library Materials Z39.48-1984.

Library of Congress Cataloging-in-Publication Data

Names: McGriff, Michael, 1976– author.
Title: Eternal sentences / Michael McGriff.
Description: Fayetteville: University of Arkansas Press, 2021. | Series:
    Miller Williams poetry series | Summary: "Eternal Sentences, winner
    of the 2021 Miller Williams Poetry Prize, bears witness to the unseen
    worlds of gravel roads, working-class families, and geographic isolation"
    —Provided by publisher.
Identifiers: LCCN 2020042490 (print) | LCCN 2020042491 (ebook) |
    ISBN 9781682261620 (paperback) | ISBN 9781610757416 (ebook)
Subjects: LCGFT: Poetry.
Classification: LCC PS3613.C4973 E84 2021 (print) | LCC PS3613.C4973
    (ebook) | DDC 811/.6—dc23
LC record available at https://lccn.loc.gov/2020042490
LC ebook record available at https://lccn.loc.gov/2020042491

Funded in part by

MILLER AND **LUCINDA WILLIAMS**
POETRY FUND

for Dorianne Laux & Joseph Millar

I adjust the time
so as to pass through my life

—Bei Dao

CONTENTS

SERIES EDITOR'S PREFACE

When the University of Arkansas Press invited me to be the editor of its annual publication prize named in honor of Miller Williams —the longtime director of the press and its poetry program—I was quick to accept. Since 1988, when he published my first full-length book, *The Apple That Astonished Paris*, I have felt keenly indebted to Miller. Among the improvements to the world made by Miller before his death in January 2015 at the age of eighty-four was his dedication to finding a place for new poets on the literary stage. In 1990, this commitment became official when the first Arkansas Poetry Prize was awarded. Fittingly, upon his retirement, the prize was renamed the Miller Williams Poetry Prize.

When Miller first spotted my poetry, I was forty-six years old with only two chapbooks to my name. Not a pretty sight. Miller was the one who carried me across that critical line, where the "unpublished poets" impatiently wait, and who made me, in one stroke, a "published poet." Funny, you never hear "unpublished novelist." I suppose if you were a novelist who remained unpublished you would stop writing novels. Not the case with many poets, including me.

Miller Williams was more than my first editor. Over the years, he and I became friends, but even more importantly, before I knew him, I knew his poems. His straightforward, sometimes folksy, sometimes witty, and always trenchant poems were to me models of how poems might sound and how they could *go*. He was one of the poets who showed me that humor had a legitimate place in poetry—that a poem could be humorous without being silly or merely comical. He also showed me that a plainspoken poem did not have to be imaginatively plain or short on surprises. He was one of my literary fathers.

Miller occupied a solid position on the American literary map, though considering his extensive career and steady poetic output, it's surprising that his poems don't enjoy even more prominence. As his daughter became the well-known singer and recording artist that she is today, Miller came to be known as the father of Lucinda Williams. Miller and Lucinda even appeared on stage together several times, performing a father-daughter act of song and poetry. In 1997, Miller came to the nation's attention when Bill Clinton chose him to be the inaugural poet for his second inauguration. The poem he wrote for that event, "Of History and Hope," is a meditation on how "we have memorized America." In turning to the children of our country, he broadens a nursery rhyme question by asking "how does *our* garden grow?" Miller knew that occasional poems, especially for occasions of such importance, are notoriously difficult—some would say impossible—to write with success. But he rose to that occasion and produced a winner. His confident reading of the poem before the nation added cultural and emotional weight to the morning's ceremony and lifted Miller Williams to a new level of popularity and respect.

Miller was pleased by public recognition. What poet is immune? At home one evening, spotting a headline in a newspaper that read POET BURNS TO BE HONORED, Miller's wife, Jordan, remarked, "They sure have your number." Of course, the article was about an annual celebration honoring Robert Burns.

Miller's true legacy lies in his teaching and his career as a poet, which covered four decades. In that time, he produced over a dozen books of his own poetry and literary theory. His poetic voice tends to be soft-spoken but can be humorous or bitingly mordant. The poems sound like speech running to a meter. And they show a courteous, engaging awareness of the presence of a reader. Miller knew that the idea behind a good poem is to make the reader feel something, rather than to merely display the poet's emotional state, which has a habit of boiling down to one of the many forms of misery. Miller also possessed the authority of experience to produce poems that were just plain wise.

With Miller's sensibility in mind, I set out to judge the first year's contest. I was on the lookout for poems that resembled Miller's. But the more I read, the more I realized that applying such narrow criteria would be selling Miller short and would not be fair to the entrants. It would make more sense to select manuscripts that Miller would enjoy reading for their own merits, not for their similarity to his own poems. That his tastes in poetry were broader than the territory of his own verse can be seen in the variety of the books he published. The list included poets as different from one another as John Ciardi and Jimmy Carter. Broadening my own field of judgment brought happy results, and I'm confident that Miller would enthusiastically approve of this year's selections— winner Michael McGriff's *Eternal Sentences*, finalist Craig Blais's *Moon News*, and finalist Madeleine Wattenberg's *I/O*—as well as those of previous years.

If I had to give a Hollywood elevator pitch on behalf of Michael McGriff's *Eternal Sentences*, the 2021 Miller Williams Poetry Prize winner, I might say that it's a blend of the low-rent sociology of Raymond Carver with the quirky imagination of Richard Brautigan. The speaker of these poems lives in the realm of Kmart, McDonald's, and Gas Qwik. Friends are in jail. A snake is coiled inside a Schlitz can, the family is too proud to accept food stamps, and the neighbors are "too poor for a fence." But that, compared to the method and power of these poems, is just the scene, not the subject.

The title of this book is very explicit about what lies inside, that is, a series of sentences. Of course, we could describe just about all writing from the Bible to Jim Thompson as a progression of sentences, but here the sentence is king. I was enjoying myself so much on first reading that I failed to notice right away the distinguishing scheme at work in every poem. Each line of every poem is its own periodic sentence, where the reader must fully stop before he or she can go on. And the period is the only punctuation allowed in this collection, apart from a handful of apostrophes just to keep track of who owns what. The comma, a useful way to guide the sentence and control its rhythm, is banned. The period rules. The deeper we wade into McGriff's collection, the more we realize that while the exclusive use of end-stopped sentences, one after the other, is the source of the poems' power, it is also a self-imposed restriction. It reminded me of W. S. Merwin's comment that he abandoned (or transcended!) punctuation in order to make writing poems more difficult for himself by doing without its help. Here, every one of McGriff's poems is a box of sentences.

Such a repetition of short, declarative sentences risks the monotony some associate with the lockstep heroic couplets of eighteenth-century English poetry. But the sentences here, for the most part, are a wonder. Whether linked to create a suggestion of a narrative or, just as commonly, to not strain toward a singular point, the stacks of sentences are always fresh and often striking. Some are straightforward:

> "I wore the same jacket to your wedding and your funeral."
> "My sandwich tastes worse than I thought."
> "They're poking at a fire with curtain rods."

Others are quirky, surrealistic:

> "A skyful of sparrows poured from my chest."
> "I try to step through a mirror discarded in an alley."
> "Three early stars torqued into place along the border."

And the hand of Brautigan is present:

> "The elk sharpen their craft of disregarding us."
> "Everyone from the eighteenth century looks seventy-five
> and doomed."

Eternal Sentences makes us reexamine the line in poetry and the sentences that lines can hold. Charles Olsen ordered that "no line must sleep." The lines gathered here could not be more aroused, aware, and wakeful. Here's one poem in its entirety:

Tonight I Am

A dead flashlight in a kitchen drawer.
A sheet of three-cent stamps.

A fistful of gravel as a last defense.
Wind against the house lying through its teeth.

This series of short sentences produces both individual eye-openers as well as some overlap that suggests possible patterns. One leaves these poems with the feeling that life comes at us in a series of sentences too stark to be interrupted by the brake-tapping of a comma. I've heard metaphors for life that hold less truth. *Eternal Sentences* will come at its readers as a series of happily endless delights.

———

To return to the elevator for a moment—*Moon News*, finalist for the 2021 Miller Williams Poetry Prize, can be seen as the unlikely marriage of Charles Bukowski and Sir Philip Sidney, but of course, that doesn't do justice to Craig Blais, who is a strong and engaging poet in his own right. We can say that *Moon News* is a collection of sonnets if we allow that a poem cast in the basic shape of a sonnet is a sonnet. The shadow of the English sonnet is visible here: fourteen lines divided into three quatrains and the couplet. But the quatrains are not grammatical units as they tend to be with the Elizabethans; rather, they run on into the next quatrain and finally into the couplet, amen. This is the more urgent, jumpy sonnet in which the poet talks through the shape of the poem, hurrying ahead until he feels the couplet nearing; then he finds a way to use the two remaining lines to close the poem up. As readers, we experience both the familiarity of the sonnet box and the many novel twists and odd surprises of this poet's original hand. In one poem, Blais's grandmother's pea soup recipe acts as the closing couplet. In other scenarios, the couplets sound like items from a police blotter or a nurse's log. This is the sonnet repurposed for our time.

Here's one example from a stack of endings. The speaker is sitting at home watching a football game and drinking "a thirty-pack" when a friend stops by and declares he is "interested in exploring 'traditional / masculine gender roles.'" And here are the lines that directly follow:

> The sun is reversing
>
> its magnetic field every eleven years—flipping
> end over end like a chariot tossed by horses
> off the road and down a rocky embankment.
> North becomes south and south north as it follows
>
> an orbit around a galaxy center that flails its arms
> like a wide receiver looking for a penalty flag.

That is not allowed in prose, and it shows Blais's full awareness of the high degree of imaginative freedom offered by poetry. To read these poems is to be both enclosed by the sonnet's chalk lines and released by the wildness of the content. The swerves of thought are not dictated by the sonnet's divisions. A poem that begins about a friend schooling the poet for his drinking ends this way: "Molten iron / converts to steel and hardens until the next thing // you know, there are 446 bridges in your city / and a weapon for every imaginable atrocity." Poems, it has been said, should at least be interesting—and these are in spades. Speaking of which, a woman reading tarot cards is "bluffing like she's in the middle of a poker game." The poet writes someone's phone number on a rock and tosses it into his backyard in case he ever locks himself out of his house; he does this because "I am scared."

Most poets in America teach. Blais is in the minority who admit the experience into their poems. In teaching Kafka's *Metamorphosis*, he deals with one student who says, "'That's weird.' / The same thing he's said all semester about everything." Another thinks Gregor—the "bug-man"—"brought it on himself somehow." Or "his family did it to him." Finally, the "weird" kid is given the couplet: "'Maybe it's not about *why*. Maybe it's about / how everybody left behind just has to deal with it.'" In another poem about teaching English, the students are unimpressed when told "that *stanza* in Italian / means *room*," so teacher tells them it really means *crime scene*.

Moon News modulates into a series of sonnets about Saint Blaise, "patron saint of animals and those suffering from throat ailments." Here reverential prayers mix with hagiographic exaggerations: "Like Jesus, Blaise walked on water, but unlike Jesus, / when he got to the center of the lake, he sat down." Another section is a kind of elegy for friend "Alex," but the tone is mixed like the tone of this whole book. The sonnet never before carried such cargo: heroin, hospital rooms, poems growing out of trees and out of a person's open hand, a flower drooping "like it could give a fuck," Jeff Bezos, Tom Brady, and SpongeBob himself.

Moon News is a dazzling collection of fully American sonnets. And if you want to get the real moon news, Blais will tell you that "the moon appeared after earth took a glancing blow / off the chin 4.5 billion years ago. // Every day since it has been tugging at our seas / like a child afraid its mother will leave."

Io, you might recall, was one of the lovers of Zeus who was turned into a heifer then back into a woman. And in *I/O*, she holds a lantern to guide a poet through a book of poems, for Madeleine Wattenberg is a votary of this goddess. Io is her confidante and confessor. It is Io to whom her letters are addressed, as if the poet had one foot in the ancient world of mythology and the other in her own time. In opening up a channel between her personal history and the age of mythology, the poet develops a private association with Io and her time. *I/O* is peppered with questions as if the poet sought answers to her own unfolding journey: "Io, tell me how you left the grove." "Tell me how you crossed the sea with only a gnat for company." "Were you surprised when Hera took you into the grove and fastened your gold collar?" The poems seem to toggle back and forth between ancient and modern realms, with the ancient world dominating the sensibility and the sound of each utterance. Even when the poet is in her own time, her language sounds vaguely elemental, as if she wants to be better understood by Io. Subtle, intentional missteps in grammar and diction signal an effort to write in a more basic English with a more ancient sound. Nature is even animated as it would be in a mythological world: "The hills shift their shadows as though swinging a load from hip to hip." Her more natural language is tinged with a delicate sensuousness. She is "careful not to tear the purple skin" of a plum. She announces that "I don't wash my hair for ten straight years / and each day the oil drips down my back." And while swimming, "Underwater, my feet / glitter like pink cities." And many of Wattenberg's poems sparkle with stunningly inventive images, as when trees spread "like tails of peacocks to the sky" or "the clouds remain closed as caskets."

Another female figure enters the scene with Margaret Cavendish, the seventeenth-century poet, scientist, and pioneer feminist who published under her own name and challenged the belief in a mechanistic world. We get a view of the duchess's complex laboratory. Cavendish appears in a poem titled "Uses for Late Frost," which recalls a scene from her groundbreaking novel *The Blazing World* in which "a merchant abducts / a daughter as she gathers / shells along the shore." The lines that follow—"They sail to where two / worlds meet"—reminded me of how Wattenberg makes the two worlds of today and ancient Greece meet through the agency of Io.

For me, the poem that best represents the strange power and imaginative pressure of this book is "Charon's Obol," in reference to the coin that those being transported to the underworld must give the ferryman. The myth serves as background and grounding wire to the poet's growing up, from her father placing on her tongue "a sliver of peach / or a white pastille . . . a homeopathic moon," to her tongue "sliding against the edges of men," including "a boy who tastes of copper." Finally, the coin becomes the obol of death. The poet practices dying by placing "a coin / across my tongue." "How can I know which boat to board," she asks in terminal confusion, "I'm just trying to pay my way." *I/O*, despite its brief title, is a book of expansive power and enviable craft.

Congratulations to all three of these poets. The University of Arkansas Press is honored to be the home for these titles for years to come.

Billy Collins

ACKNOWLEDGMENTS

Thanks to the editors at *Terrain*, where "1995," "Eminent Domain," "Neighbors," and "No Bond, No Levy" appeared previously.

To the collective vision of Billy Collins, the late Miller Williams, Lucinda Williams, and the University of Arkansas Press, I offer my sincere gratitude. Additional thanks to Janet Foxman for her editorial and aesthetic acumen.

For enduring friendships, my warmest thanks to Gray Jones, Marcus Jackson, Noah Falck, Richie Hofmann, Andy Grace, Josh Tyree, Matthew Dickman, Michael Dickman, Joseph Millar, Dorianne Laux, and Margot Volem.

To the late Eavan Boland, fiercest advocate, who made my world larger in so many ways: Thank you.

ETERNAL SENTENCES

Eternal Sentences

A motion beneath the pond scum.
I know how the moon got its black eye.
I heard it happen last night.
It transpired in the wind.
Crows as pure as lies were involved.
They factor into the wind's accent.
My father throws a fouled spark plug in the millpond.
Then another.
And another.
He cut a slit in the fence to get us here.
It was like stepping through a gill.
A catfish is more like a crow than anything else.
It is carbureted.
It runs rich.
It throws a tail of blue smoke.
Anyone worth half a shit can take one apart.
He tells me the thistle holds milk in its eye.
Just the way a catfish does.
What are you doing.
I'm feeding the fish.
He says watch this.
I smell oil and gas.
He walks off toward the black shape of the wind.

Solstice

I waken to the tongue-clicks of a new season.
Where trees use their final ten-dollar words.
The gray teeth of the morning are too busy to complain.
Flat sky an afterthought of the hangdog moon.
As a child I wore my dead cousin's pressed white shirts.
I could see in the dark and a bit beyond it.
There was no turnstile I couldn't squeeze through without paying.

Waiting for the Heat to Break into Rain

Bindweed lies flat in the ditch.
The whole county has water on the knee.
I wire my shadow to a fence.
I hear the pattern for a burial dress move through the sky.
A child pulls a shad from still water.
If only I could unsee the marquee of his face.
The molted head falls apart in his hands.

1995

Today is like yesterday.
The courthouse fills up.
We wait to be called before the judge.
We learn of each other's crimes.
We answer questions.
The judge laughs at a woman.
She stole a three-pack of boys' underwear from Kmart.
The electrician left his girlfriend's kids in the back of his car.
He had to make a quick deposit at the bank.
He left the windows cracked.
But not enough for a hand to get in.
He was only gone a few minutes.
I drank too much and pissed against a bank's picture window.
This was after my friend hanged himself.
Maybe it was the same bank.
Bodies became things they were never supposed to be.
I agree to pick up trash on the side of the highway.
I go back to work moving boxes around in a walk-in freezer.
Sometimes I turn out the lights and harmonize with the compressor.
Someday we'll colonize the moon.
I wonder if it will have pioneer graveyards filled with the names of
    children.
The ones who died at birth or never grew old enough to speak.

South Fork of Coos River

You ask a serious question and I ignore you.
I can't stop thinking about lying on the dead grass back home.
How the turkey vultures became parenthetical.
When I got up my shadow remained fastened to the ground.
It must have felt like a pile of clothes warming on the rocks.
Right after you strip them off and throw yourself to the leeches.

Elk in the Field

When I was six the elk came.
They left swirls of blue light where they rested.
Their calls were thin old women blowing on cutgrass.
After they left we took their places.
We called the matted-down grass a ghost nest.
It stayed warm there for hours.
The sun drank little bits of us.
I remember the black teeth of one man.
He split wood for our cedar fence.
He told us everything we did was bad luck.
He opened wide.
He said how do you think I got this way.

1987

The night runs up its tab.
The creek's so low it barely complains.
It smells like a burrow of dead snakes.
Horseflies set up shop.
The men call Reagan a broke-dick dog.
They're poking at a fire with curtain rods.
We burn trash in the yard.
My grandmother drinks whiskey once a year.
She considers the owls the broken teeth of the dead.

Cousin

I called you cousin my whole life.
It's confusing what you actually were.
Blood gets that way.
Like salting the sky.
Or debating who owns the moon.
I wore the same jacket to your wedding and your funeral.
On both occasions the women looked older than they should.
The same one refolded my pocket square.
Each time she said you were too smart for such a mess.
A skyful of sparrows poured from my chest.

Dead Crow's Monologue

I am packed tight in the oils of sleep.
My body unravels and can be heard in every world but this.
Certain mutinies I carry with me.
The millpond refusing to hold still for the garish wrist of the moon.
As in life my voice is a district where I don't yet exist.
Whatever leans on me with its dark shoulder is existence enough.

Mikey's in Jail

They caught him on camera.
They showed it on TV.
He shouldered in the door at Gas Qwik.
He took a package of diapers.
He took a log of Kodiak.
He emptied his pockets.
He left what he had on the counter.
As he ran through the store a freezer door opened.
Small handprints flared up on the glass.
The camera doesn't lie the State will say.
Mikey will say it sure as hell don't.

Sleeping beside the Alsea

In two more breaths the river will change direction with the tide.
The elk sharpen their craft of disregarding us.
On the far shore they are both memory and experience.
The light makes me think of a clean ashtray on a windowsill.
The wind undresses across the water.
It has never lied about what it doesn't know.

August Poem for Bei Dao

I try to step through a mirror discarded in an alley.
A dog tied to a loose railing laughs at me with a human voice.
It's impossibly early for snow.
But my footprints tell another story.

Food Stamps

She'd push the cart until there was an empty checkout line.
To make sure no one saw her take them from her purse.
She made a game of it.
She called it circling the airport.
If you think this was my mother then I dare you to prove it.
You've never actually seen her.
Not even close.

What Gets Seen

I see the crows go for something.
I forget how fast they are when it counts.
Their sound is a black ribbon torn from a dream.
Tonight it's bluegrass at the Elks.
My grandmother was buried in her Old Time Fiddlers vest.
That was some time ago.
Back when crawdads boiled on all four burners.
Back when she always looked down the well.
I wonder if it sang back.
I hear the ticker tape of the stink bugs' legs.
The night thick with ratty stars.
I'm a dusty boot print in a hotel lobby.
A water skipper's the only thing left of this memory.
In a crow I see a long string wound tighter after it's plucked.

Campaign Promises

Follow me and the ocean will become a polished wheel.
The dead will form a line to comb their hair in its reflection.
They will leave boxes of lost photographs at your door.
They will cast a bell and erect it on the grounds of City Hall.
It will ring for hours with a single strike.
A fire will burn on the edge of town.
It will belong to a kind of factory.
Its sole purpose will be to throw steep light across the landscape.
The dead will work there.
They will earn a reputation as keepers of their appointments.
They will be celebrated with mayoral declarations.
Those who die young will be particularly suited to this labor.
They will require few breaks and no water.
Small hands make quick work of many things.

Lunch Break in the Cab of My Truck

Georgia-Pacific Veneer.
My first week on the day shift.
The brackish light grown immense.
I root for an old woman crossing four lanes of highway traffic.
Or maybe it's an empty garbage bag tumbling in the wind.
The varnish has disappeared from my life.
I read a Chinese poem about a strand of silver hair.
For a thousand years it's held a bridge together.
Soldiers on horseback spark across it.
Nothing else happens.
I've lived here for twenty-six years.
Not once have I seen a man look up at the noon air-raid siren.

Concession Speech

Tonight I feel like a hired funeral mourner.
Like those potted cactuses for sale at the Gas n Go.
I'm tired of pretending I don't shop there for dinner.

Upriver Memory and Pinochle

The adults drank and smoked.
Two decks of cards.
The deep stain of kitchen light.
I slept beneath the table.
The fog was a dead woman's nightgown.
The bets elaborate as splintered chicken bone.
I heard the brittle stars in their voices.
The season lost a good eye in a fair fight.
My grandmother remembered a field.
Where she burned her clothes the year they got electric light.
Back then the wind on the river was a feather.
A feather dried fast to a butcher's sleeve.

The Last Poem about the Moon

It's doing a strange trick to the glass doors of the hutch.
Earlier I saw one black horse become two.
Each had the same patch of moon on its forehead.
They looked at me from the low end of the field.
Water gathers there and fights to obscure the stars all winter.
Soon I'll go through a dead man's pockets for the first time.

Whale

Terry cut the jawbone from a beached whale.

He got in there with a chainsaw.

We called him chicken fucker.

He drove it around on his flatbed.

It eventually shrunk down.

He could fit a whole cue ball in his mouth.

Unholy moon.

Entire face a socket.

The jawbone stopped smelling in 1992.

That's when he buried it.

He said no one should look upon God's floating rib.

On the Grande Ronde

I try to remember the rules.
Three rings around the moon is bad luck.
One means a ghost tends a fire in your shadow.
Two and you see only what the dead see.
Perhaps it's best to enter sleep with few beliefs.
And to awaken with fewer still.

The Evening

My father's hip waders dry in the breeze.
He clips his toenails over an opened newspaper.
I swam downstream from the chrome plant all day.
We sit on the porch and don't say much.
The wasps grow tired in the creek's long hours.
The moon no longer has a Secretary of War.
Now we call it the Minister of Condolences.

Tonight I Am

A dead flashlight in a kitchen drawer.
A sheet of three-cent stamps.
A fistful of gravel as a last defense.
Wind against the house lying through its teeth.

Eminent Domain

I'm worthless at sharpening a chainsaw.
Even with a vise and a good file.
My cuts smoke and pull hard to the left.
I thin the property.
The County says we need papers for our spring water.
Tests and permits.
The State says get a lawyer.
The stumps I leave behind are shaped like tire chocks.
Not even the drunkest ghost will stop to tie his shoe on them.
When the pipeline's surveyors trespass I slash their tires.
I paint my face and disappear into the woods.
I fire rock salt through the trees.
We tell the deputy we haven't seen shit.
The moon's behind on its rent.
It hasn't opened its mail in a year.
As soon as the rain comes we'll burn our brush in the field.
There are so many arguments against us.
And no map to carry the runoff of our voices.
Not a line not a name not a legend.

County Clerk's Office

The courthouse has been falling apart for thirty years.
The roosting crows on the pioneer statues are beautifully indifferent.
A woman adds her name to my document with shaky blue hands.

Driving by Johanson's

His light goes on for the first time this winter.
I see it from the dike road.
It could be thieves.
A gathering.
A twist of sky off the floodplains.
I wonder if I care.
The hour between hours.
I'm driving to sober up.
I fell asleep earlier watching public television.
A child in a desert looked into the camera and was counting.
Her language a hull in deep water.
She was still counting when I came to.
Johanson's window.
The color an oil furnace whispers in a cellar.
The light moves from room to room.
Does it follow Johanson or does he follow it.
Suddenly the world darkens like gravel in the rain.

Presidio

White crosses in a field of white gravel.
Three early stars torqued into place along the border.
I offer here my best translation of a young mother's grave.
There are colors one comes to think of as memory.

Westport Ferry

There's no light that requires us.
I step into an hour of steady whitecaps.
Leeward a voice a door a rotten beam.
Perhaps I'll regather my shadow on the far shore.
Without entirely succeeding.

1986

I took a knife to school.
On the morning bus ride I'd sharpened it with spit and a rock.
I cut the Levi's tag from Christian's denim jacket.
I couldn't say all the months in a row.
I couldn't spell remember or narwhal.
At night my mother set up her sewing machine on the counter.
She attached the tiny red flag to my jacket.
She didn't say whatever it takes.
She didn't say anything at all.

Aging

Near the end I'll make a nest from a clump of your dark hair.
I'll fish it from the drain with a bent hanger.
Near the end I'll forget your name.
The same way I no longer hear the gate moaning on its last hinge.

Side Work

Jorge leans on his shovel.
A spool of wire gone crazy at his feet.
The shadow-scramble among the scrub.
The sun deals in absolutes.
My post-hole digger hits pure clay.
The river's become a field of dry rocks.
The new signs call it Wolf Creek.
We call it the Devil's Thumb.
The clay is gray streaked with orange.
Clouds name their children after it.
It belongs to the same dream as Tessa Muldova's hair.

Ontological Tire Shop

At Steady Tire we stand on opposite sides of the front door.
I pull and she pulls and nothing moves.
I have a child screaming at my side.
This moment becomes a strand of bells clanging against the glass.
They could belong to a camel but never will.
Like all fathers I am a failure.
I'm a fiction that exists between a horse and a stand of white pines.

Idiot Tax

I buy five lottery tickets at the Gas Qwik.

The jackpot's 600 million.

We say more money than God.

It's been all over the news.

A stranger in line tells me I'm paying the idiot tax.

How to explain that I'm actually buying tickets to the past.

Every Saturday we ate a take-n-bake pizza.

We talked into the night about what we'd buy one another.

My father my mother my sister and I.

Because you understand nothing about the poor.

I must lie to you.

It's the only way.

I say I grew up on food stamps.

But that isn't true.

My mother was too proud for that.

Instead we grew thin and cold and I fought everyone.

Even now when I meet a new person I visualize striking them
   in the throat.

We've paid the idiot tax all our lives.

I am we are a runnel for such light.

I'm two swings ahead of what happens next.

Trading Places with the Moon

It's a catalog of common bewilderments.
Whereas I'm a hero for simply walking through a field.
We play these roles until last call.
Then switch back.
I take the long way home along the river.
I piss on a mailbox and put the flag up.
The trees wear white gloves and reach into the water.

Neighbors

The night dries out in the still hours of the ravine.
I sit in the kitchen with the lights off and the windows open.
Too late to go to bed.
Too early to get ready for work.
Tracy came over after dinner and said Janet was back in jail.
Skipped on her parole officer and stole some groceries.
We looked at our feet and kicked the gravel for a while.
Someone at work will say they saw this coming.
Now the alder shadows spread into the cups and bowls.
The houses the outbuildings the barns.
They crouch on their haunches and groan.
They are old men at a funeral waiting to see who will speak first.

In the Hayloft Looking East

The rat and I share a cigarette while a hopeless star registers a complaint.

A Job Up North

The only drinking water comes from Larry's well.
This time of year it goes warm and tastes of crab shells.
The black pitcher pump resembles a torn-up calf's leg.
When Larry's around he walks among the animals.
A blue star clings to a branch.
God's earring.
A sign we'll get shorted $500 at the end of the season.
And take our money with few complaints.

Election Year

The night sky.
What the hell do I know about it.
In my truck the radio pundits quote the famous dead.
I haven't had a drink in over two years.
I could never find my way by the stars.
The moon skulks around the crepe myrtle.
It's been kicking dents in my aluminum downspouts.
It stares into water in a way the men in my life have perfected.
It's drafted years of intricate plans for a boat it can never afford
   to build.

Five Translations of Morning Light

Everyone from the eighteenth century looks seventy-five
    and doomed.
Something with three remaining breaths in the blue shadow
    of the oak tree.
To aggravate my neighbor I roll the garbage can to the street
    in the nude.
"A CandleLion Poem" by Richard Brautigan makes me
    irreversibly seen.
The flowers begin to open like drowned kings.

It's the First Day of Burn Season

I've got some diesel and lawn chairs.
Our pile of dead lumber and windfall is ready to go.
I walk down the road to Don and Carla's.
I invite them over to drink and watch it.
They are too poor for a fence.
They use pallets with rebar and baling wire instead.
I say looks like you about got it done.
Don puts his arm around Carla's waist.
Says hell.
This is a crab pot for them crooked little angels.

Antonio Porchia

All morning I thought of your dead translators.
The sound of a dented tuba in an alley.
A cloud looks like a ghost barking demands in an unfurnished room.
The cloud wavers across the brass.
Remember me they say to each other.

Inventing the Cyclops

We drove to town and idled in parking lots.
I took several face punches at the 7-Eleven.
We got on the CB to chase down what was next.
Kmart McDonald's wherever.
Back then I stayed in front of the narrative.
I said you should've seen how I held him down.
How I crushed my cigarette between his eyes.
Later I'll come to understand something about defeat.
How predictable it is.
How common.
How like a crow when it shifts from purple to black and back.
Now flies swirl to life in my footprints.
I'm waiting to understand the green lake only a blind child can see.

Calm Seas

Which means I must set my voice across the water.
Breaking trail in the blue snow is similar to this joy.
Someday I'll fail to read a tape measure.
The sudden arithmetic of the trees will frighten me.
For now crows fighting over a stick give birth to me in this light.
Light is another word for water looking to find its form.

A Visitation

The distance between all things is somehow this hour.
In the mirror I see it pressed to my face.
A strip of cellophane from a pack of smokes.
No it's the membrane over a fish's eye.
But there is no mirror.
Just this ghost crouched over me.
Like a canyon in a green hour it says what do you remember.
It touches my forehead with its lips.
Says nothing stays lost forever.

Self-Portrait in October Light

The shadow of my right arm against the barn floor.
It could be a motionless tail covered in horseflies.
Or the shape inside the executioner who's just used his final sick day.
Any moment a rat will step onto it.
And assess its worth before returning to the wall.

Elegy for A. C. with Water and Anwar

The lungs fill until we hear them.
We call it water but mean pulmonary edema.
We mean dying but say labored breathing.
I wasn't there when A. C. crawled to the headwaters of his shadow.
Five hundred miles stood between us.
I was pulled to the side of the road near Barrow Draw.
The sky a mess of dreams and red thorns.
Half of me tracking a movement in the scrub.
Half of me reading the poems of Chairil Anwar.
Who in 1949 wrote *The taste of the sea has changed.*
I said A. C. and meant it.
I said river and the clouds grew heavy.
Just as the taste of the sea had changed.

De Profundis

A living man and a dead man.
These are the same man regardless of the light.
Again he's brought us together.
My friend and me.
We translate the past six years for each other.
It's snowing.
It's September.
Sons have grown estranged.
Parents have entered the final pages of so many ledgers.
Outside our window children walk into the street.
They begin to eat from the ground.

1999

In the break room at Building 2.
Poplar shadows the length of memory tangle at the windows.
Stan yammers on about Zeno's Paradoxes.
Al says you talk to a cop like that you'll never get out of a ticket.
Probably get you hog-tied.
My sandwich tastes worse than I thought.
The county fair's in town.
None of us are going who don't have kids.
The strange feather of my thought falls into the landscape.
Stan says motion is just an illusion.
We stagger back to the line.
The veneer's still hot when it reaches my station.
I smooth putty into knotholes.
My guardian angel never wears earplugs.
Sometimes we stand toe to toe.
He makes my shadow dance to the beat of the sorter.
When yelled at he simply smiles.
He understands nothing and agrees to everything.
He's grown deaf and unseen and perfect.

Ambush

My friend slides the legs of his daughter's crib into green mason jars.
To keep the scorpions from climbing up.
To catch the good light from the hills of central Texas.
When I turned forty-three I began seeing spots.
I tell my son they are fireflies made of glass.
I'm caught in a valley of smoke swarmed by tracer rounds.

No Bond, No Levy

They closed all the country schools that summer.
Ours was beyond the pavement where the gravel begins.
Roads with numbers instead of names.
They said we could keep any books we wanted from the school
    library.
In July the fire department burned it down for practice.
We sat on the tailgate and watched.
It was like reversing the footage of a horse rising to its feet.
Come September we got bussed into town.
I fought every kid who laughed at my green rubber boots.
I'm home now and it's low tide.
I haven't spoken aloud in two days.
Black water falls apart against the jetty.
Like the long ash of my grandmother's cigarettes.
How doomed to the obvious water makes me feel.
How seen-through I've become.
The ocean so unlike us.
It only lives in the present tense.
When I was nine I rebuilt the carburetor in my dirt bike.
I forgot to repack a tiny spring into a chamber of its aluminum
    heart.
Muddy smoke followed me.
My name became fouled.
I cleaned it with gas and a rag.
I held it wide open until the piston warped.
Until nothing looked the same.

Approaching with Marvel

To a portion of a coyote in the new snow.
I didn't realize it was you dragging yourself in circles.
At that distance your screams were eternal.
You looked like a child with an uncommon sense of style.

Certain Images and Not Others

A snake coiled in a Schlitz can as one example.
But not a mushroom cloud in a desert.
Nor a statue weeping blood along the border.
When the snake emerged it was impossibly long.
It stretched across the gravel road.
From ditch to ditch.
It became a fissure a child must leap.
The milk thistle knew its name.
No nothing happened after that.
It's forever what must be crossed to be understood.
Now I turn out the lights and sit by the window.
The moon guides my shadow by the elbow.
I listen to the trees breathe.
I ask the landscape for a sign.
Nothing folds into nothing.

Roadside Cross

I am two sticks.
A white bird divides me.
I am bridled.
I empty into myself.
I am not quite the rain.

Record Lows

The parking lot iced over with no reflections.
The gas cap won't turn.
I remove a glove.
A greased-up moon.
Branches shatter and fall through the minutes.
Parts of my hand tear off.
I think of a mooring cleat and the sound of blackened rope.
A power line goes down.
It's a gleaming tray of instruments.
Soon I will be made to speak.

First Meditation in the New Year

The roads become impassable.
My friend dies near the end of his long sentence.
The snowdrifts reach toward the eaves.
As dimensionless as a shadow streaked across the lake.
A word repeated until it carries weight but no meaning.
I say his name when the light is right.
And the light is always right.

Decreation

The sun moves east.
A mare reunites with her shadow.
I've yet to describe this life as a crate of oily rags.
The County calls back its surveyor.
He removes the map from our Chevy's warm hood.
Water circles back to water.
There's no need yet to summon our final words.

NOTES

The formal element in *Eternal Sentences* is indebted, in part, to Larry Brown's short story "Boy and Dog" from *Facing the Music* (Algonquin Books, 1988).

The epigraph is the refrain from Bei Dao's poem "Along the Way," which appears in *Old Snow*, translated by Bonnie S. McDougall and Chen Maiping (New Directions, 1991).

"Whale" is for Stephan Torre.

"Presidio" is for Tim Johnson and Caitlin Murray.

"Five Translations of Morning Light": Richard Brautigan's "A CandleLion Poem" appears in *The Pill Versus the Springhill Mine Disaster* (Dell Publishing Company, 1968).

"Antonio Porchia": Porchia (1885–1968) was an Argentine poet known for his book of aphorisms, *Voices*, notably translated by W. S. Merwin (Big Table Publishing Company, 1969).

"Elegy for A. C. with Water and Anwar": Chairil Anwar (1922–1949) was an Indonesian poet, notably translated by Burton Raffel in *The Complete Poetry and Prose of Chairil Anwar* (SUNY Press, 1970).

"Roadside Cross" is for Gregory Orr.

"Ambush" is for Beau Thorne.